T0045557

60 PROGRESSIVE PIANO PIECES

You Like to Play

ED. 1617

ISBN 978-0-7935-2573-7

G. SCHIRMER, *Inc.*

7777 W. Bluemound Rd. P.O. Box 13819 Milwaukee, WI 53213

ALPHABETICAL INDEX BY COMPOSER

ALPHABETICAL INDEX BY TITLE

In May

Franz Behr, Op. 575, No. 2

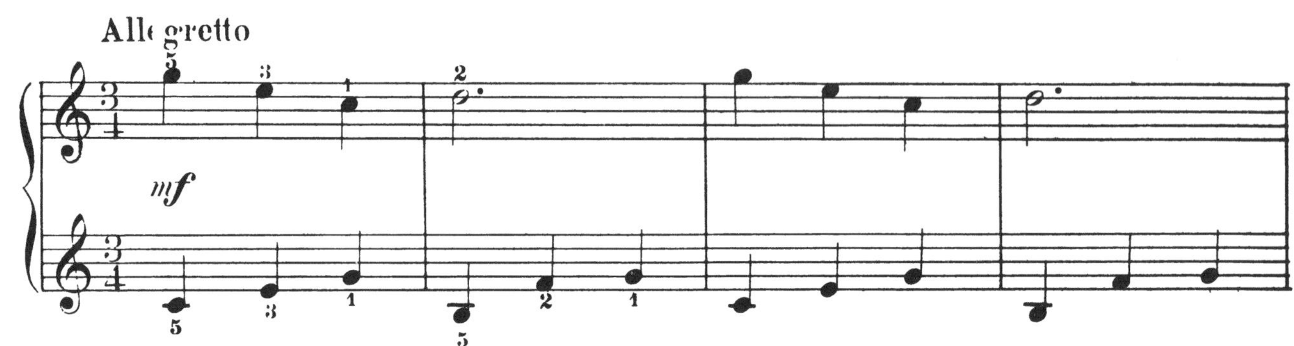

The Clock

Ada Richter

Allegretto ♩= 96
p
All day long the clock goes tick! tock!
p

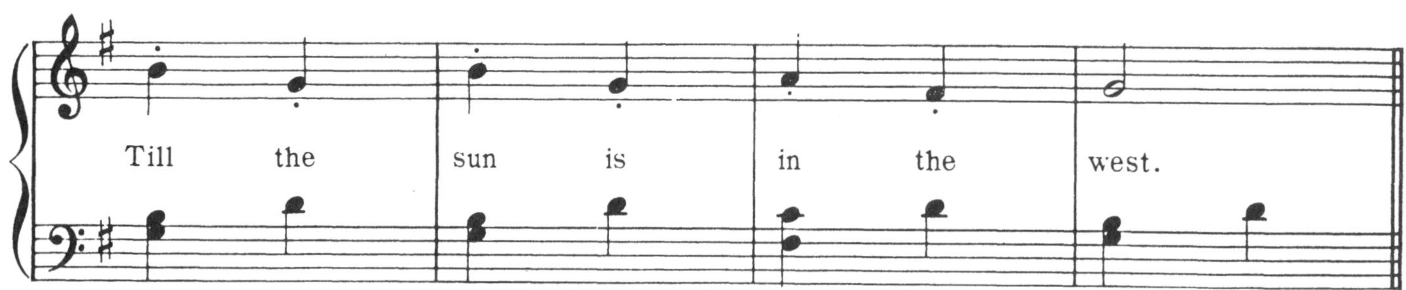

Till the sun is in the west.

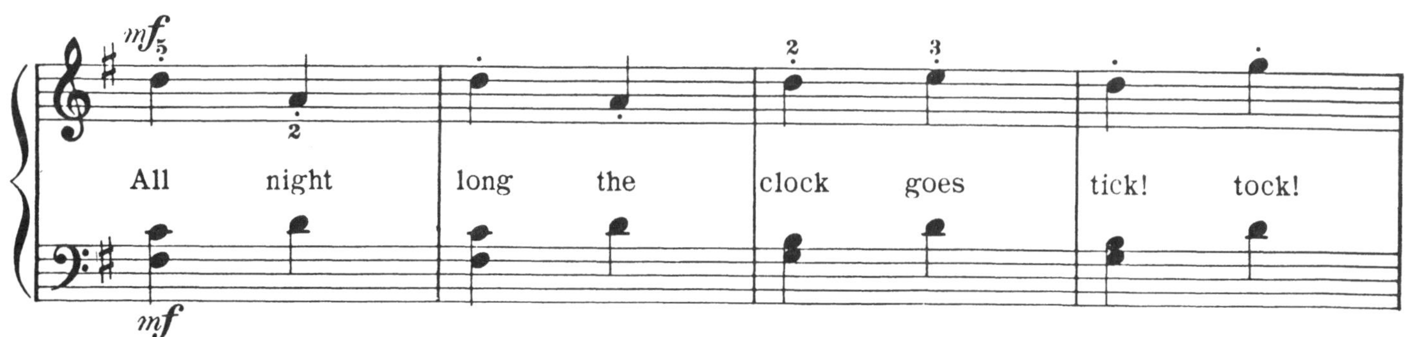

mf
All night long the clock goes tick! tock!
mf

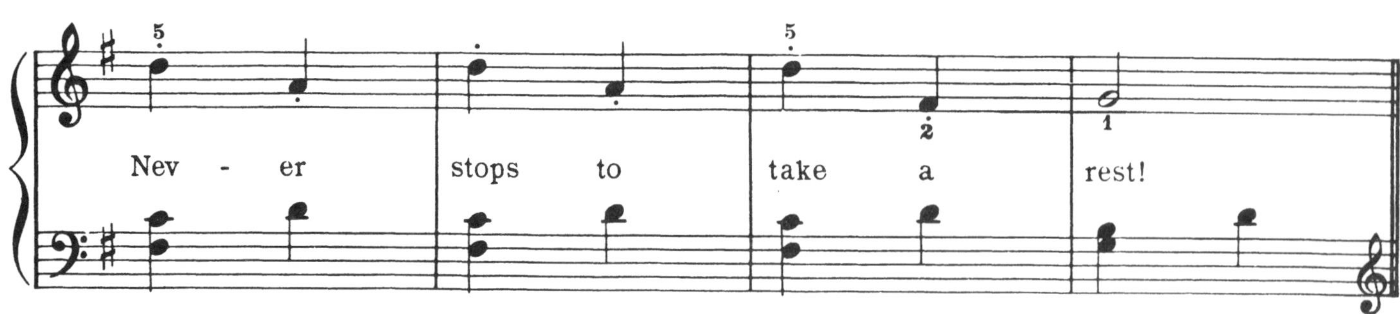

Nev - er stops to take a rest!

Andante ♩= 72
Hear
chimes
ring,
How
they
sing!

Tempo I°

Andante
Dawn
is
here!

Copy-Cat

Audelle Alford Thompson

f
mp
mf
mp
slower
f

Woodland Waltz

Francis Gwynn

p
mf
pp
cresc.
mf

The Snake Charmer

William O. Munn

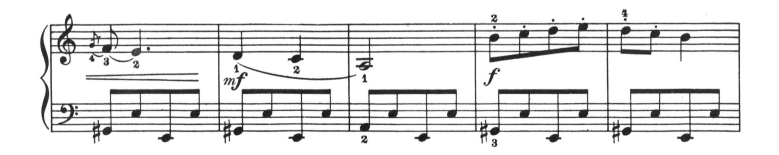

p
f
p
f
p
f
p
f
p
pp

Minuet

J. S. Bach

Allegro (♩ = 144)

mf

p

cresc.

f

Soldiers' March

Munter und straff.
Allegro deciso. (♩ = 120)

Robert Schumann, Op. 68, No. 2

Minuet No. 1

Edited and fingered by
John D. Hazen

W. A. Mozart

This Minuet and Trio were composed by Mozart in 1761, the fifth year of the composer's age

To my pupil- Lester Rainwater

Parade of the Midgets

Elizabeth L. Hopson

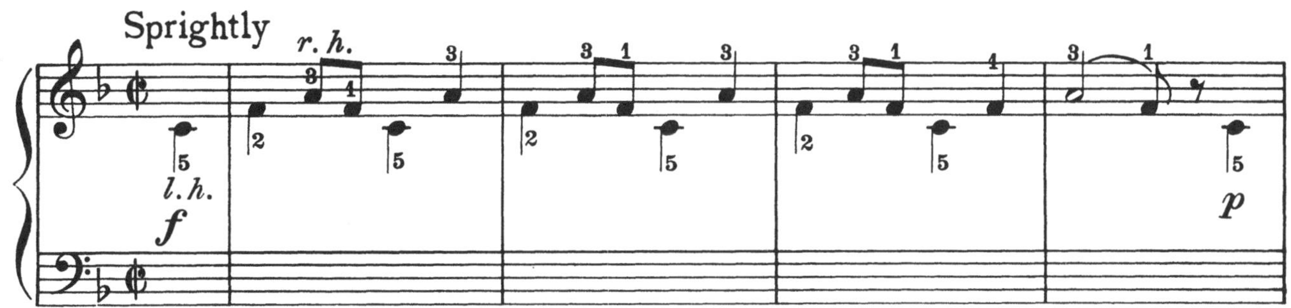

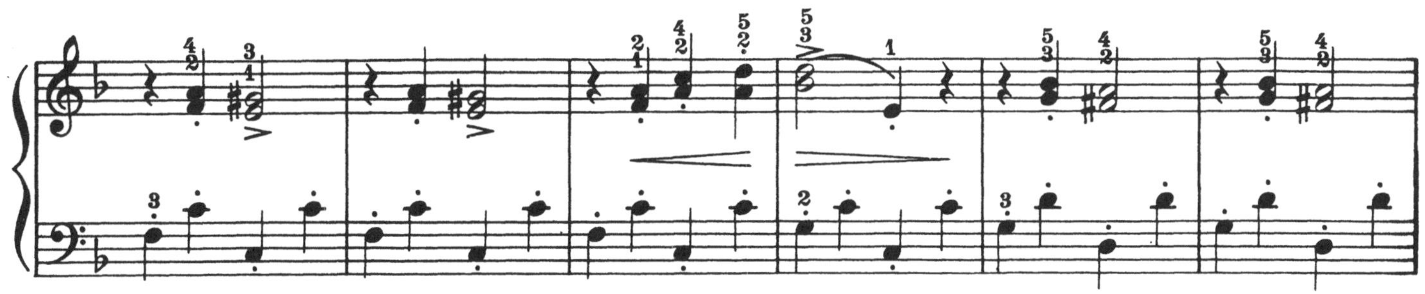

p

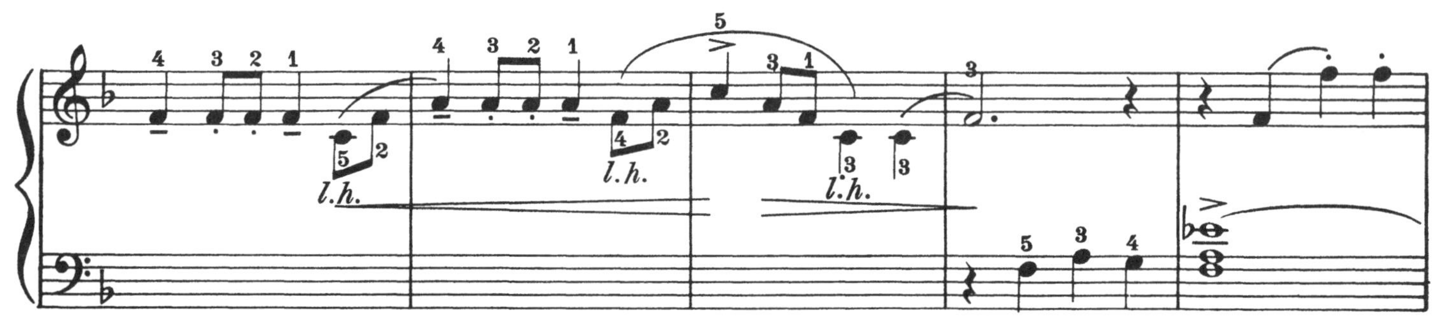
l.h.
l.h.
l.h.

l.h.
l.h.

f
p

mf
f
l.h.
p
pp
ppp
fz

Sonatina No. 1
in G

Revised and fingered by
Wm Scharfenberg.

Ludwig van Beethoven

Romanza

Allegretto (♩. = 76)

For Frank Pilling

Indian Drum

Katherine K. Davis

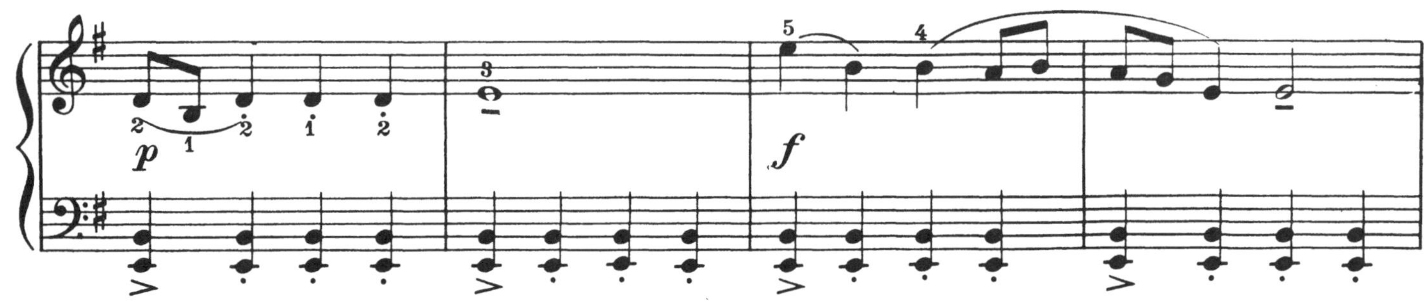

*The left-hand part is played an octave lower than it is printed.

p
f
p
p
p
pp

The Merry Farmer

Robert Schumann, Op. 68, No. 10

Waltz

N. Louise Wright. Op. 32

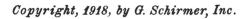

a tempo
p
cantabile
mf
p
mf
f
p
p
f
p
poco rit.

a tempo
p
Ped.
Ped.
Ped. simile
mf
poco rit.
a tempo
p
f
rit. e dim.
pp
Ped.

Dreamland

Poem by
Rosalyn Greene

Music by
Katherine Allan Lively

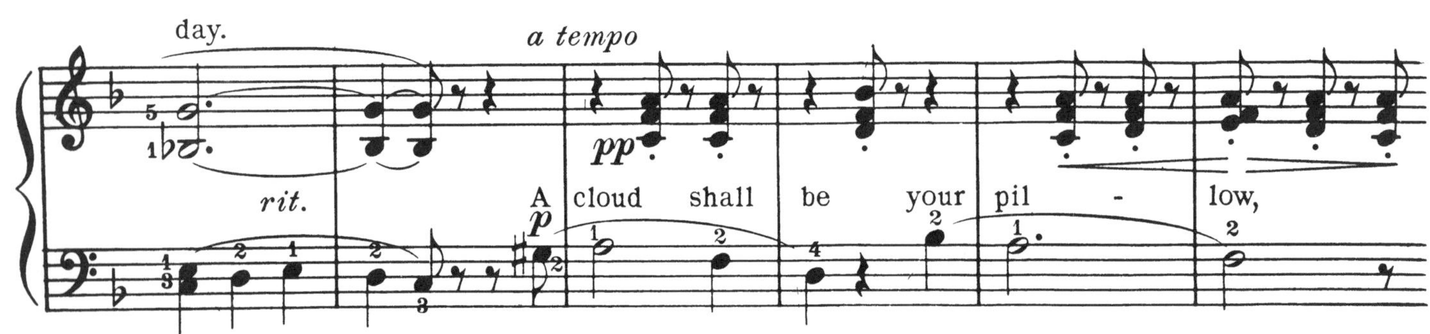

A star your can - dle - light:
Sweet
dreams un - til I (we) meet you
In the mag - ic
land of night,
Sweet dreams un - til I (we)
meet you
In the mag - ic land of night.
f
p
poco rit.
più lento
lento
a tempo
rit.
pp

The Wild Horseman

Robert Schumann, Op.68, Nº 8

To Dorothey Madtson

The Swimming Pool

Swimming lazily in the clear water

Myra Adler

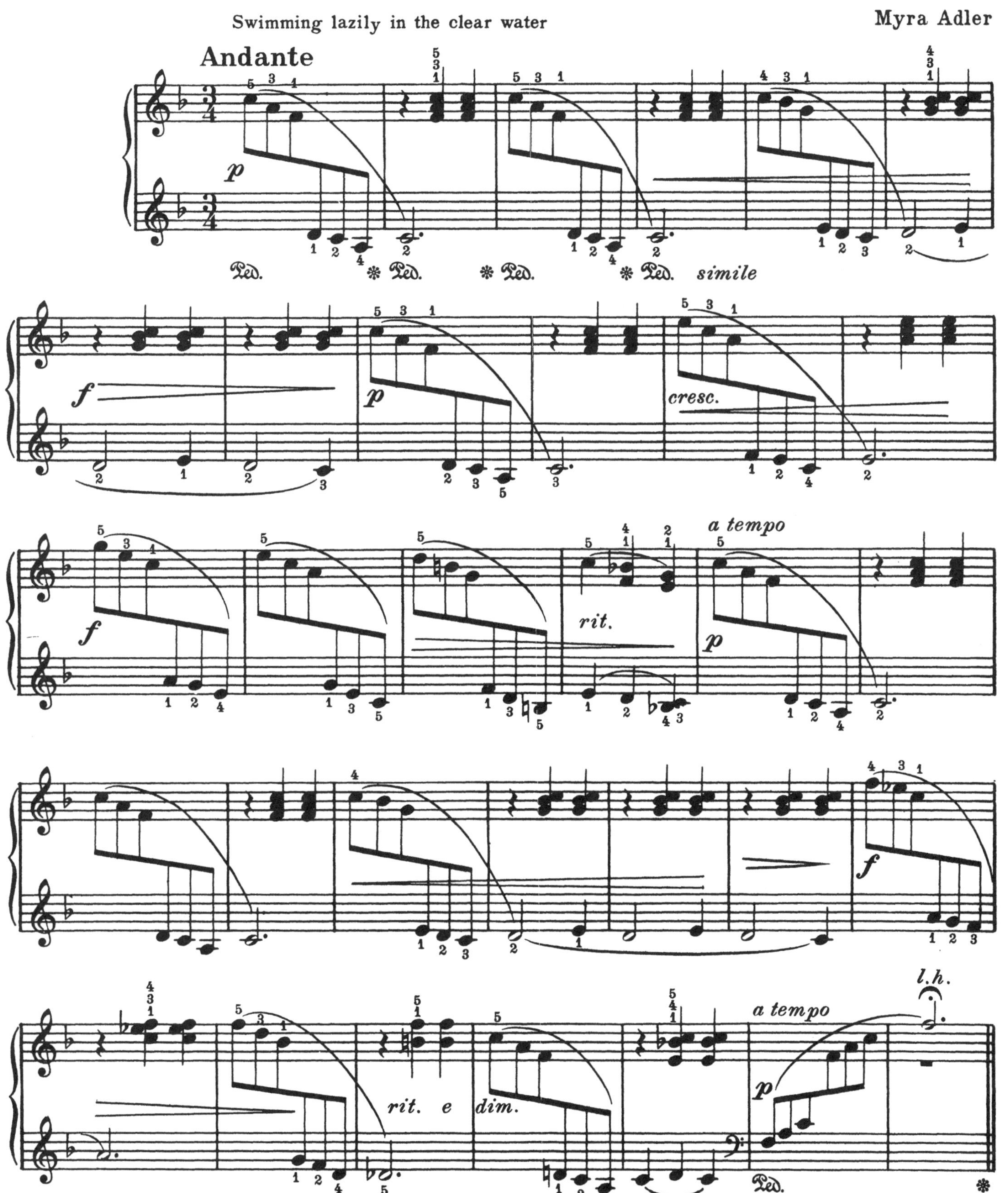

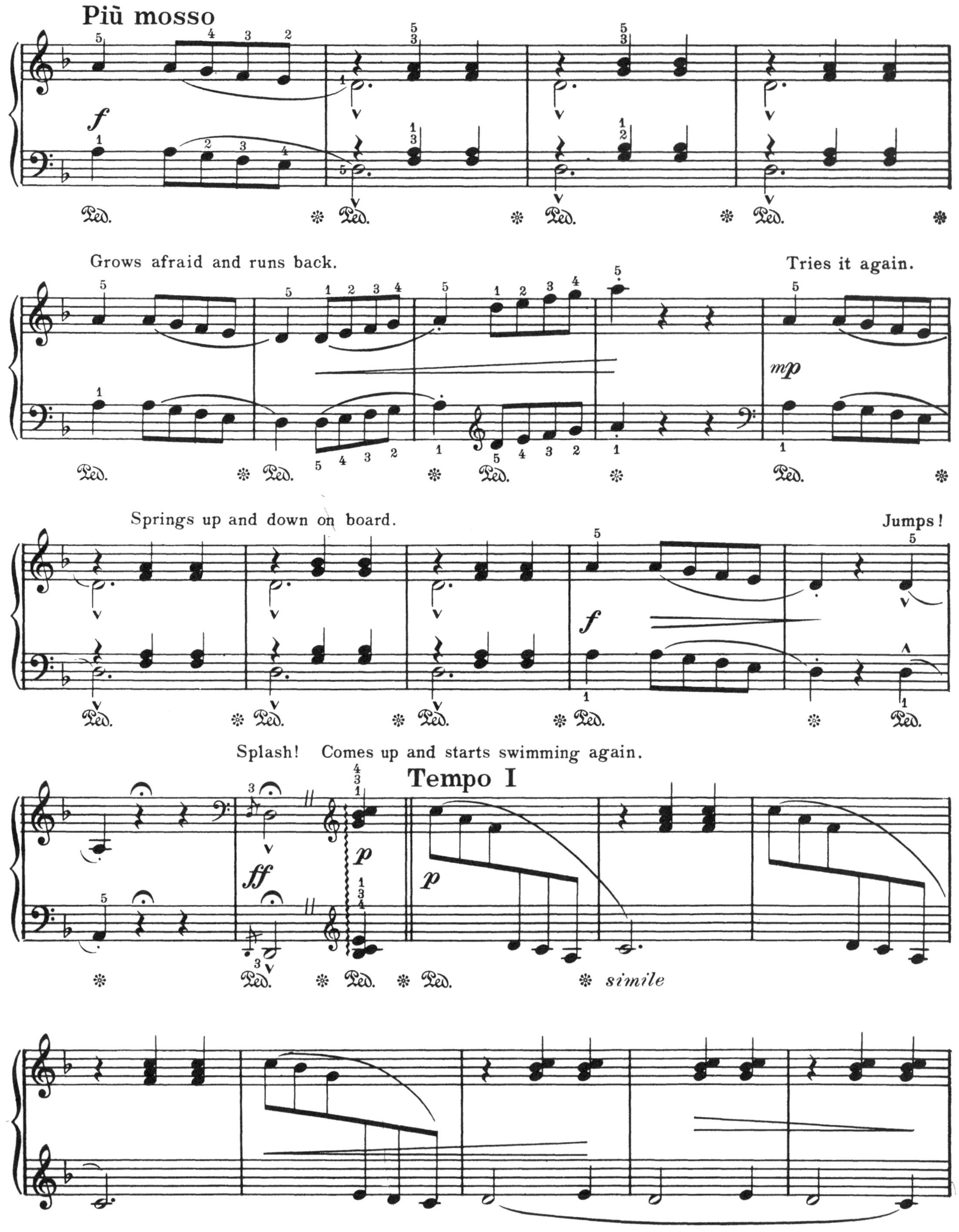
Runs out on the diving board. Springs up and down on it.
Più mosso
Grows afraid and runs back.
Tries it again.
Springs up and down on board.
Jumps!
Splash! Comes up and starts swimming again.
Tempo I
simile

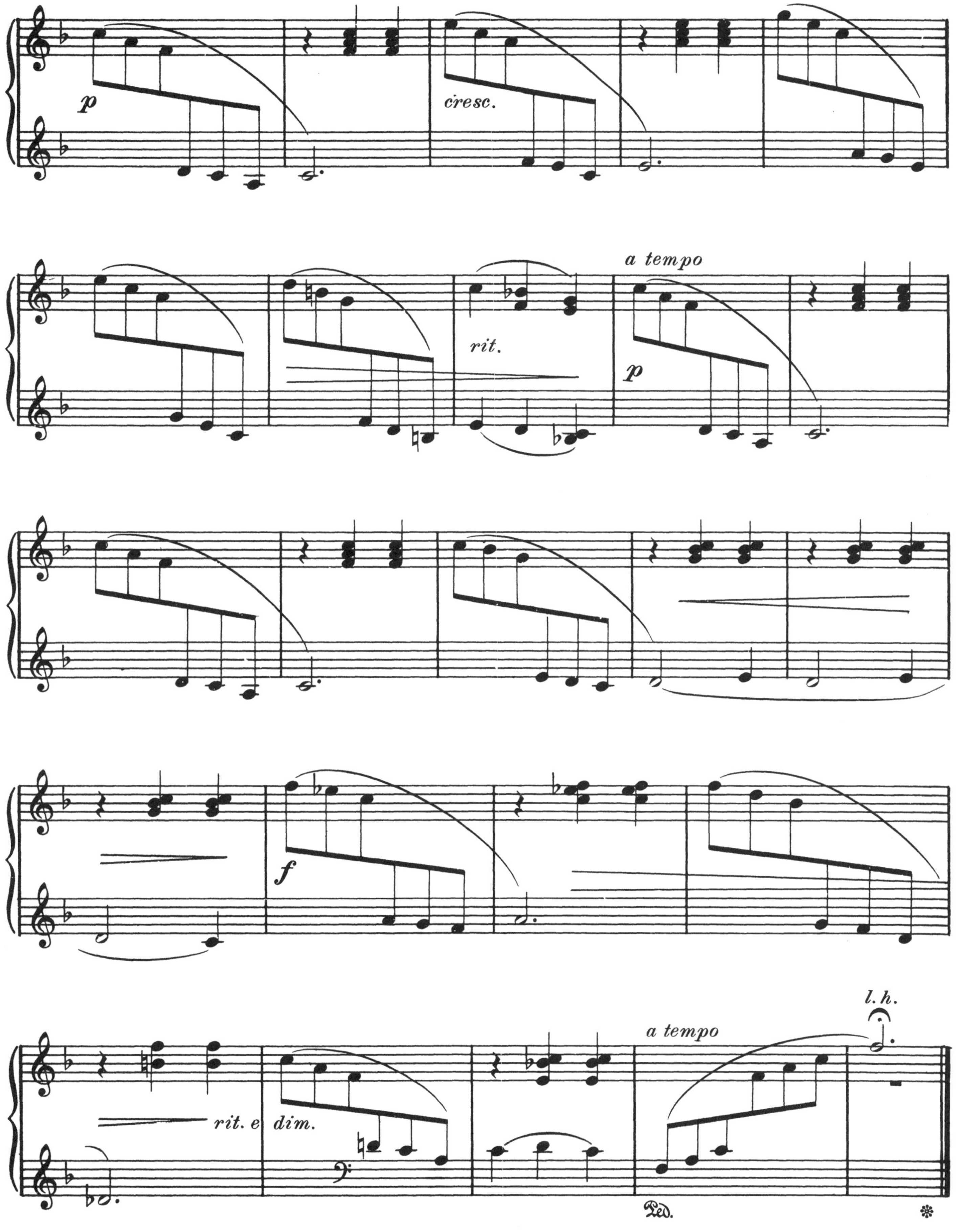
p
cresc.
a tempo
rit.
p
f
l. h.
rit. e dim.
a tempo
Ped.

L'Avalanche

Stephen Heller

mf
p
cresc.
cresc.
f
mf
p
f
risoluto.
fp
p
cresc.
8
p
sf
1
p
1

Around the Hills

MABEL LEWIS CASE

rit.
a tempo.
cresc.
loco

Edited and fingered by
Louis Oesterle

Prelude

(No. 1, from Well-tempered Clavichord)

J. S. BACH

pp
cresc.
dim.
pp
cresc.
f
ff
dim.
p
pp
ca - - - lan - - - do

Spooks

You will hear ghost stories
Thrilling you through,
And then witches and spooks
Will be spoken of too;
But don't be afraid
It's all done in fun,
For twilight's the time
When these tales are spun.

Maxwell Eckstein

dim.
8va bassa ad lib.
rit.

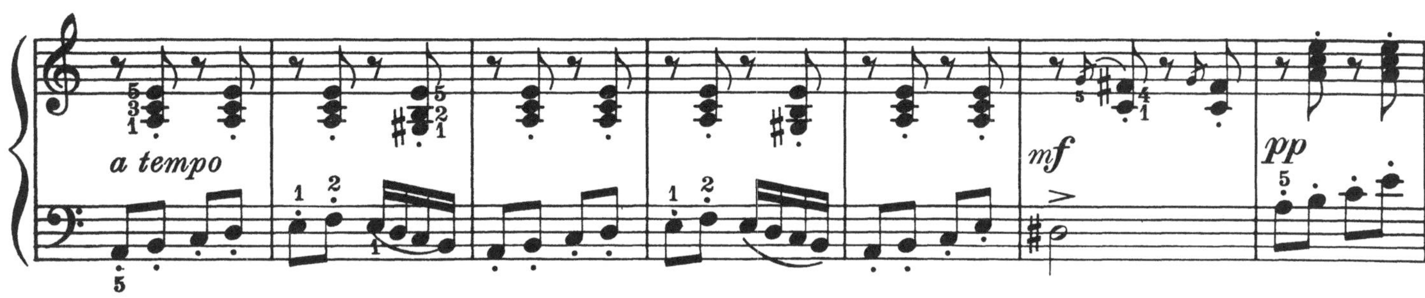
a tempo
mf
pp

mf

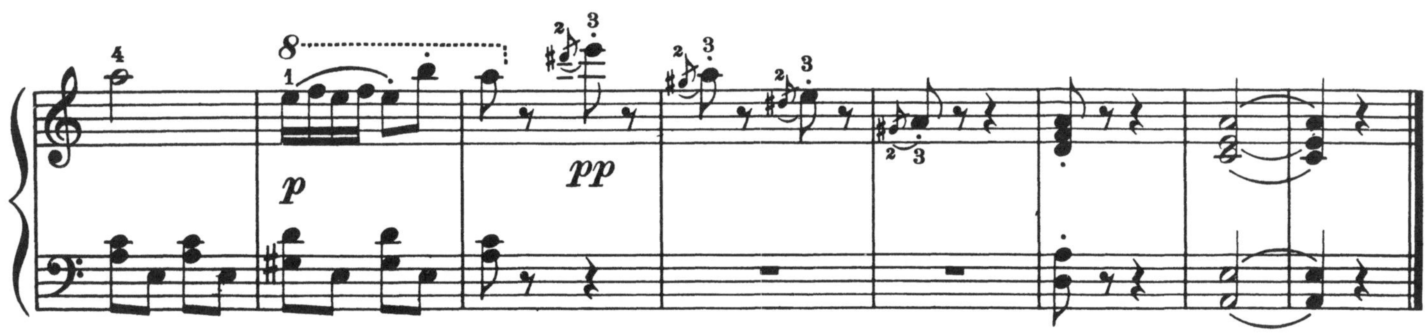
p
pp

Spinning Song
(Spinnliedchen)

Edited and fingered by
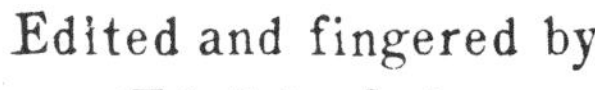

ALBERT ELLMENREICH. Op. 14, No 4.

cresc.
p
cresc.
p
legg.
cre
scen
do
f
p cre
scen
do
poco rit.
a tempo.
p
rit.

The Waterfall

(Arpeggio Waltz)

Marie Hobson

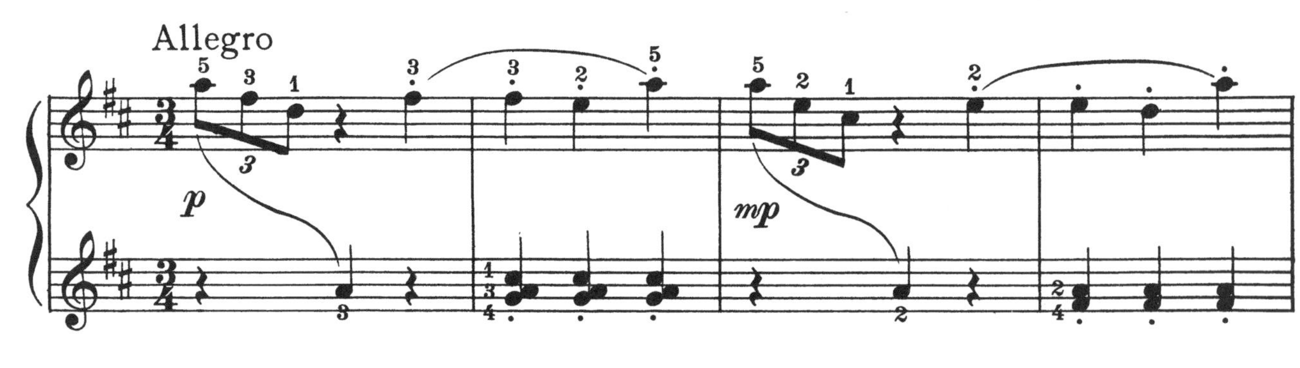

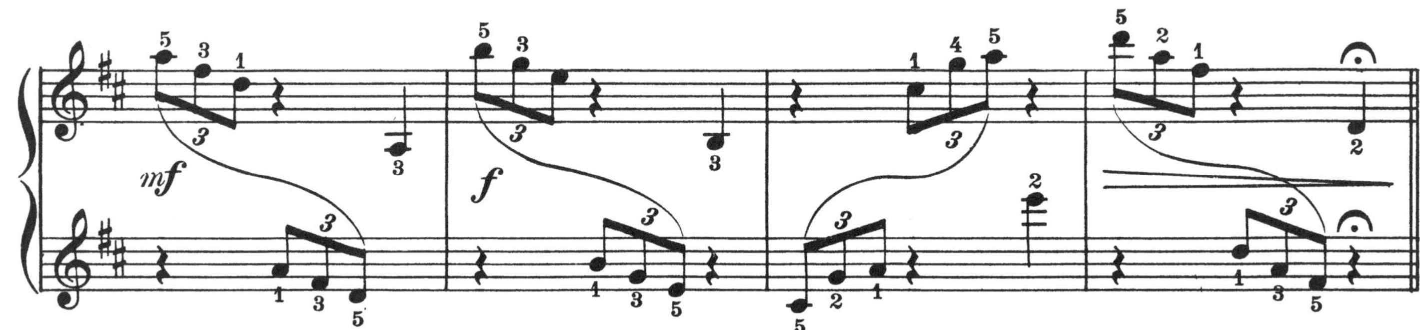

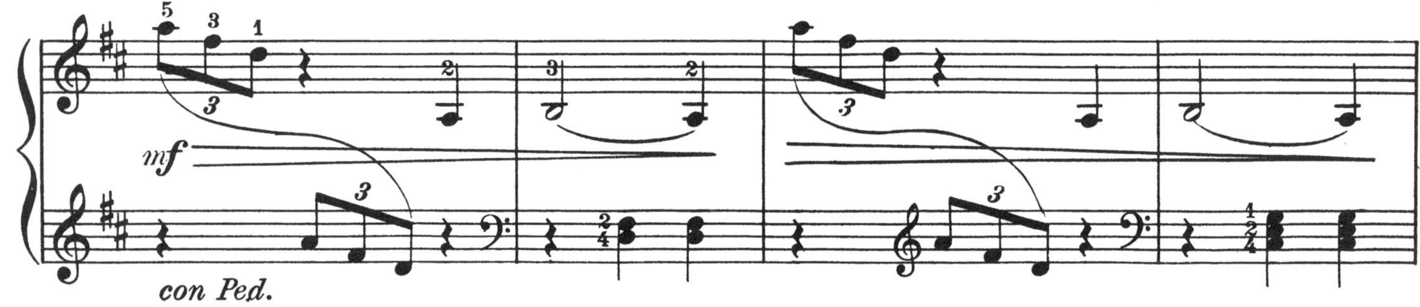

mf
p
l.h.
pp
ritard.
ppp
a tempo
mp
l.h.
pp
l.h.
mf

f
mp
f
cresc.
ff
8va
8va

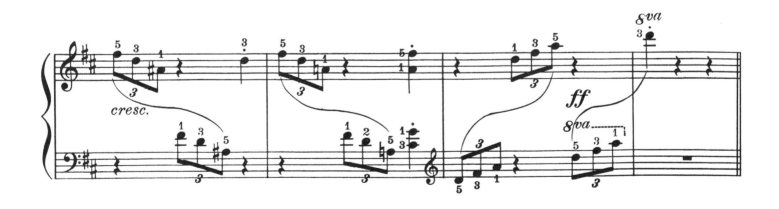

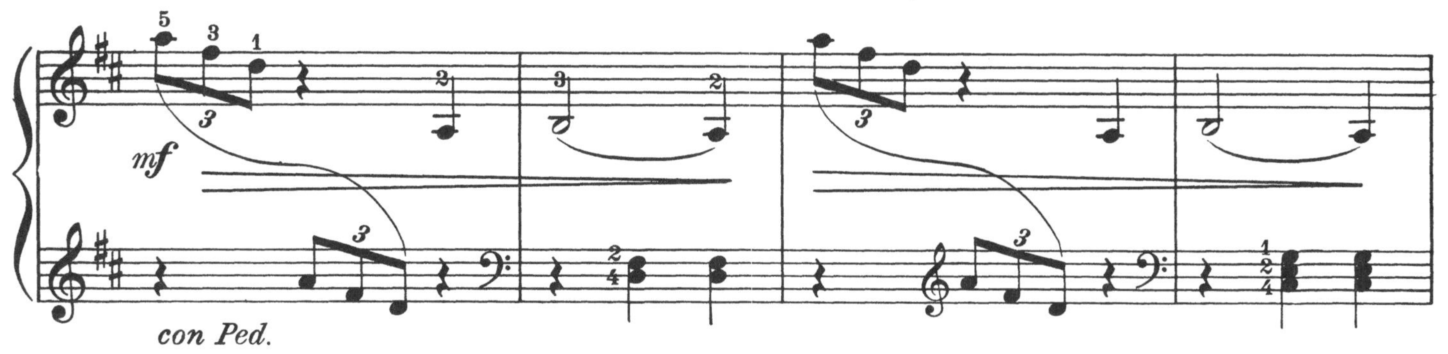
mf
con Ped.

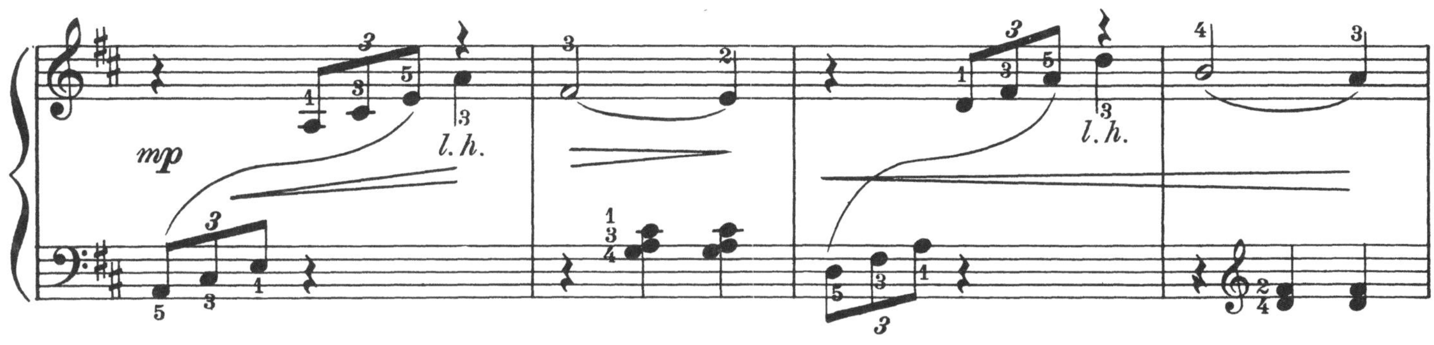
mp
l.h.
l.h.

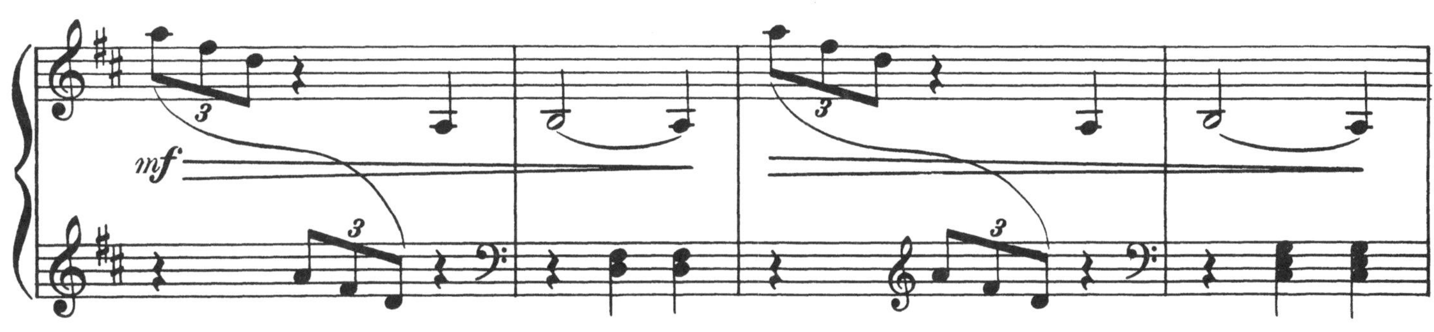
mf

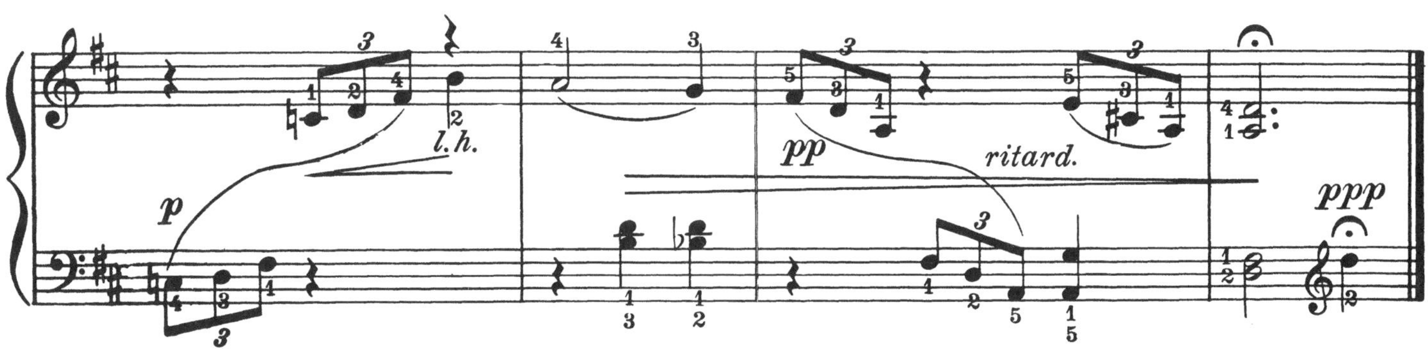
p
l.h.
pp
ritard.
ppp

Minuet in G

Edited and fingered by
Carl Deis

Ludwig van Beethoven

mf
f
(p subito 2da volta)
p
f
mf
sf
f

Swinging in Fairyland

Oh, who is so merry, so airy, heigh ho!
As the light-headed fairy? Heigh ho,
Heigh ho!
His nectar he sips
From the primroses' lips
With a hey and a heigh and a ho!

Author unknown

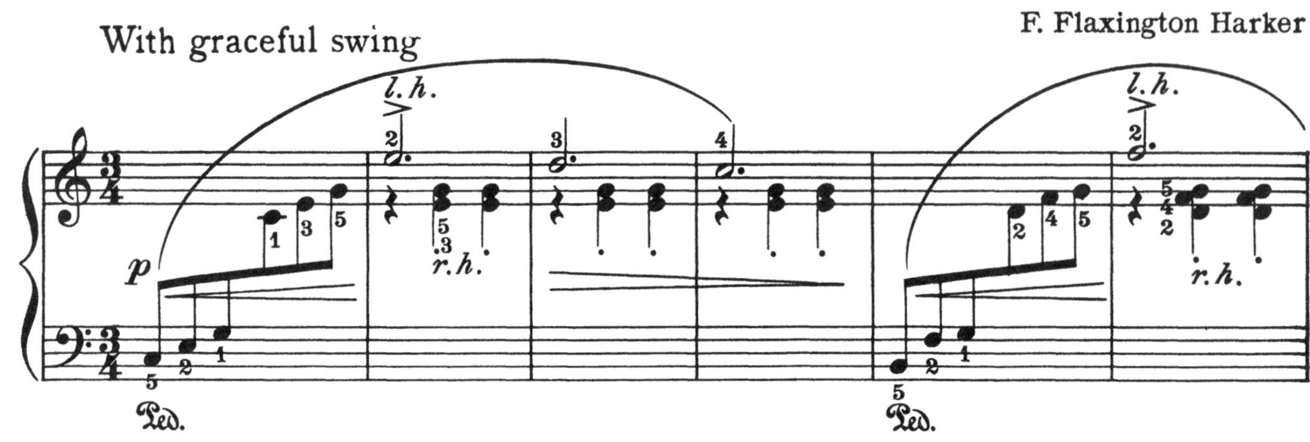

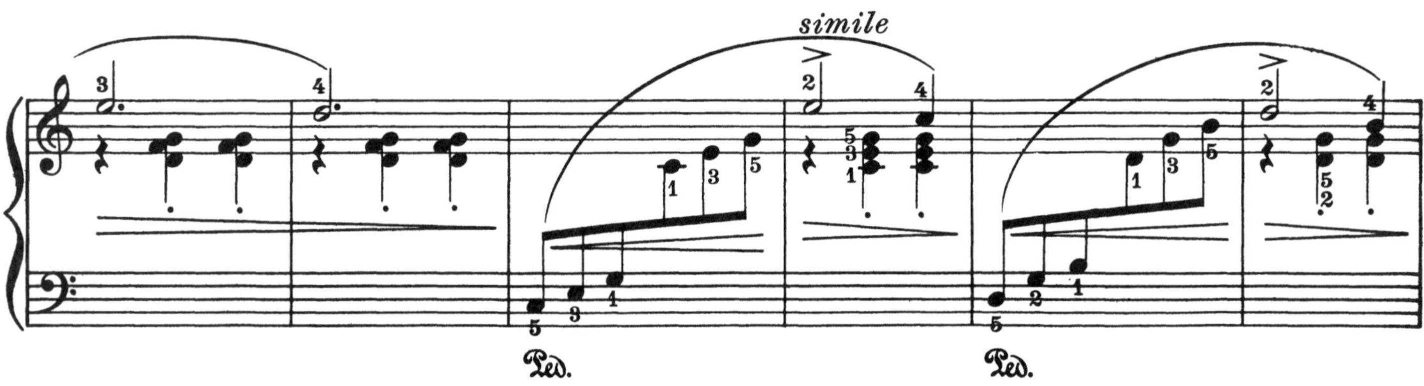

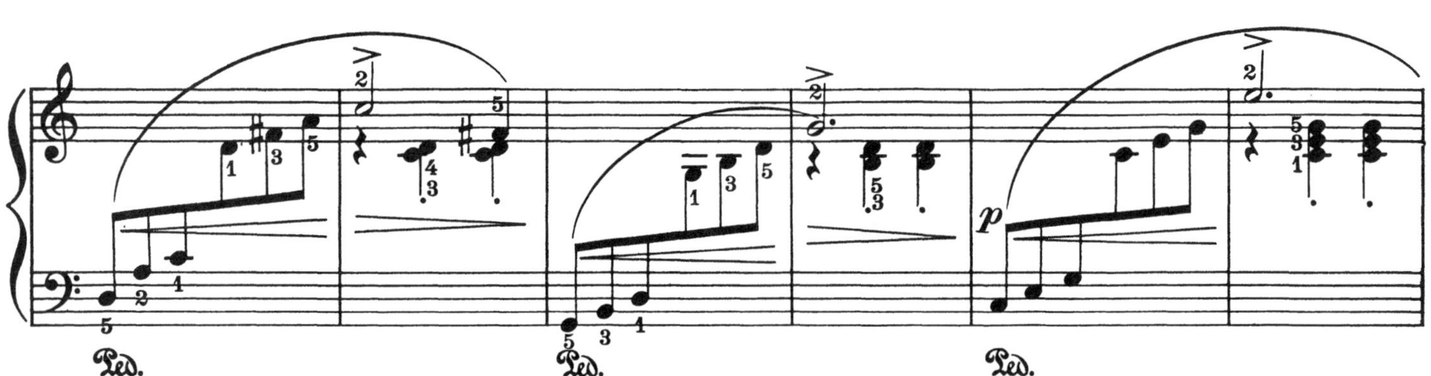

mf
Ped.
f
l. h.
r. h.
p
cresc.
ff
rall.

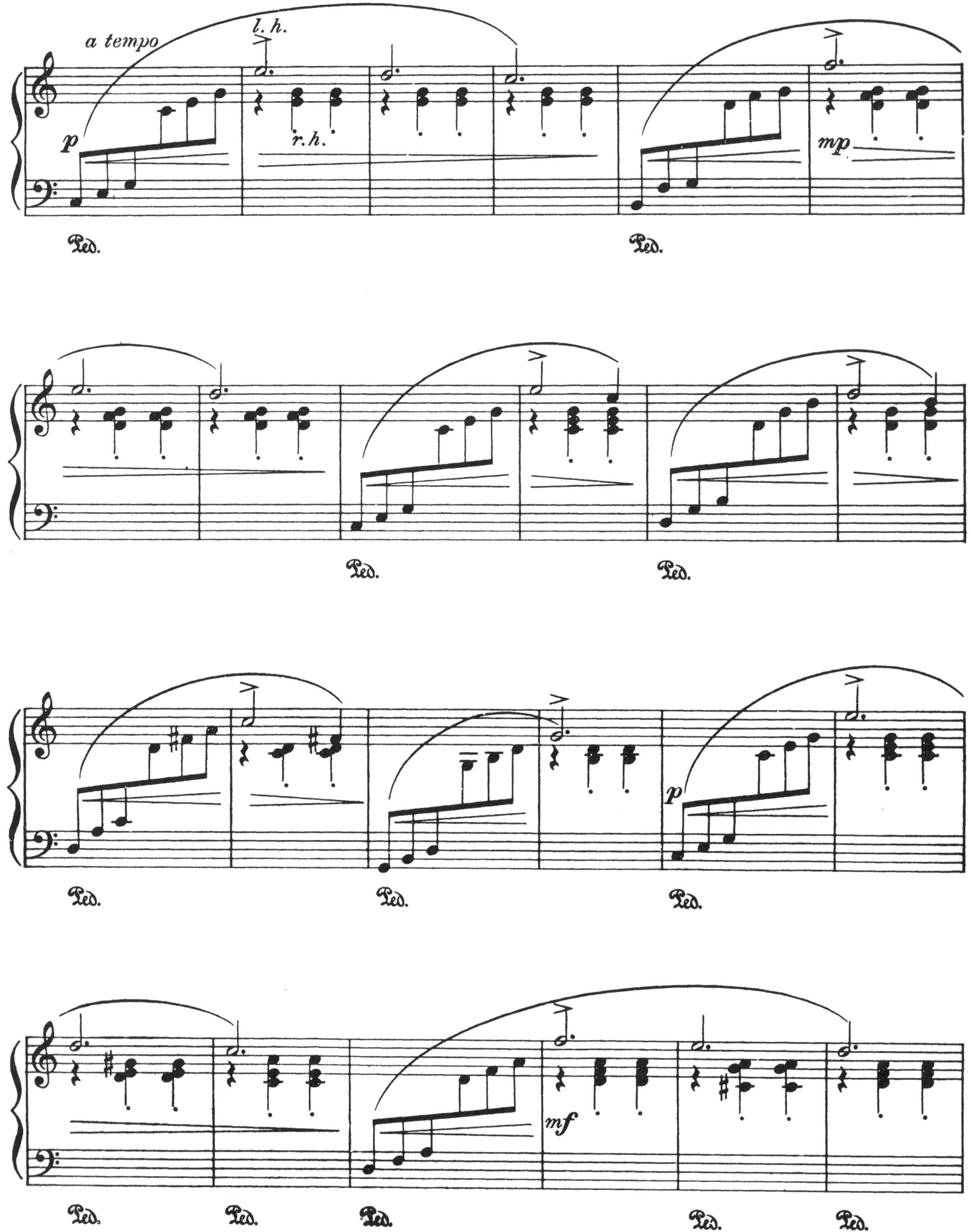
a tempo
l. h.
p
r. h.
Ped.
mp
Ped.
Ped.
Ped.
Ped.
Ped.
p
Ped.
Ped.
Ped.
Ped.
mf
Ped.
Ped.

Ped.
f
Ped.
mf
Ped.
l. h.
r. h.
f
8
f
8
rit.
p
ppp

A Melody

After Mendelssohn

N. Louise Wright. Op. 34

p
Ped.
Ped.
Ped.

cresc.
Ped.
Ped.
Ped.

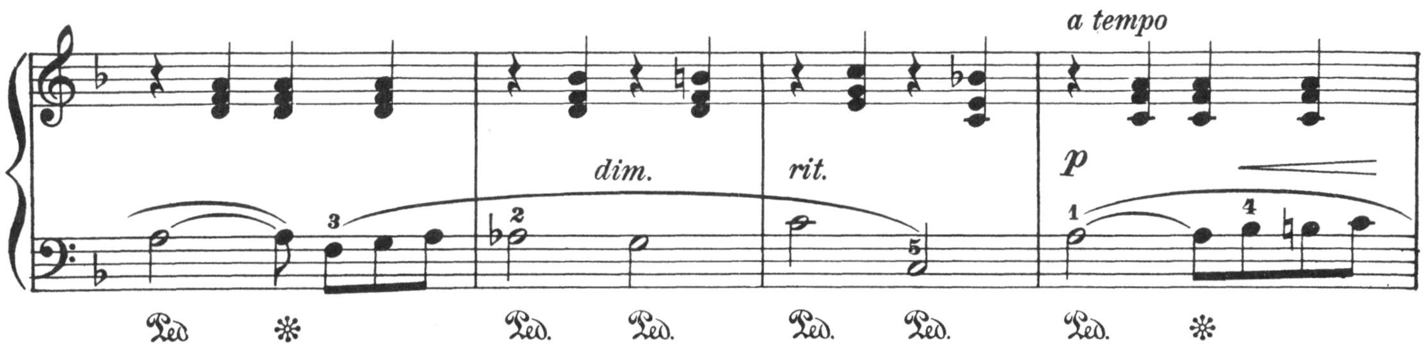
a tempo
dim.
rit.
p
Ped
Ped.
Ped.
Ped.
Ped.
Ped.

Ped.
Ped.

Ped.
Ped.

Ped.
Ped.
Ped.

p
dim.
Ped.
Ped.
Ped.

pp
rit. ppp
Ped.
Ped.
Ped.
Ped.

Sonatina

Muzio Clementi, Op. 36, No. 1

Andante.
dolce
cresc.
cresc.
dolce
dolce
Vivace

p
f
p
f
dimin.
p
pp
f
f
p
f
ff

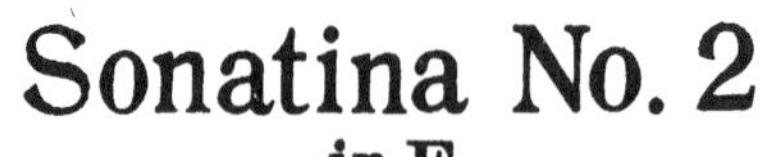

Sonatina No. 2
in F

Revised and fingered by
Wm. Scharfenberg.

Ludwig van Beethoven

Allegro assai.

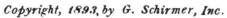

f
dim.
p
f
dolce.
cresc.
f

Rondo.

Allegro.

mf
p
cresc.
ad lib.
a tempo.
p
mf
p
mf
p
f

Veil Dance

N. Louise Wright

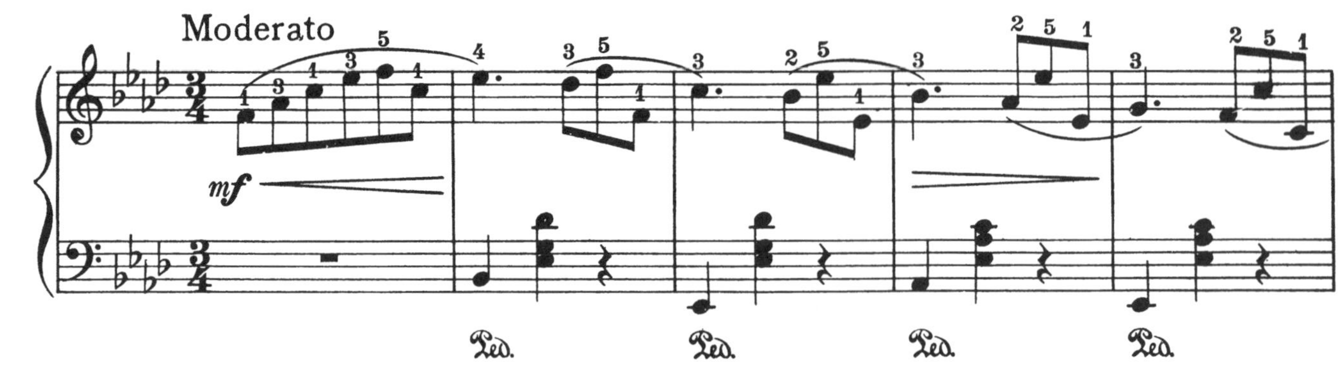

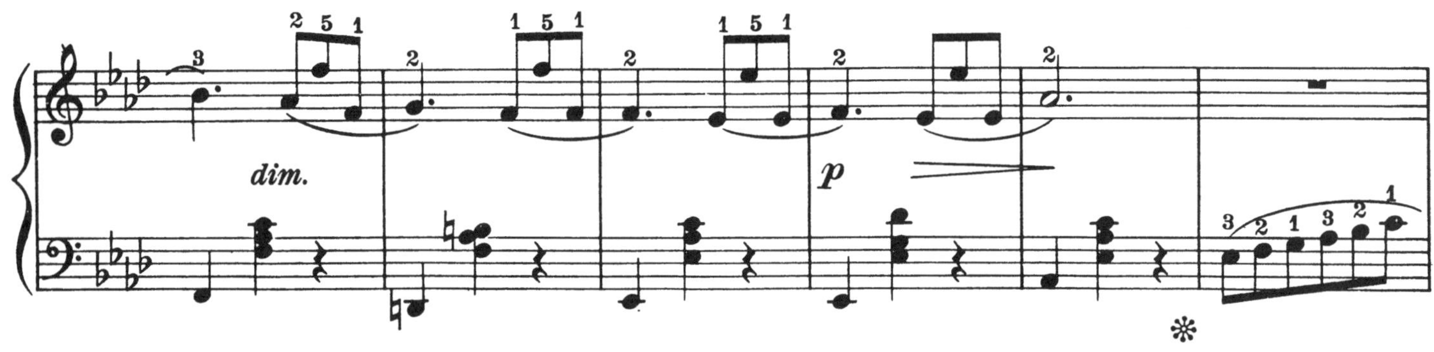

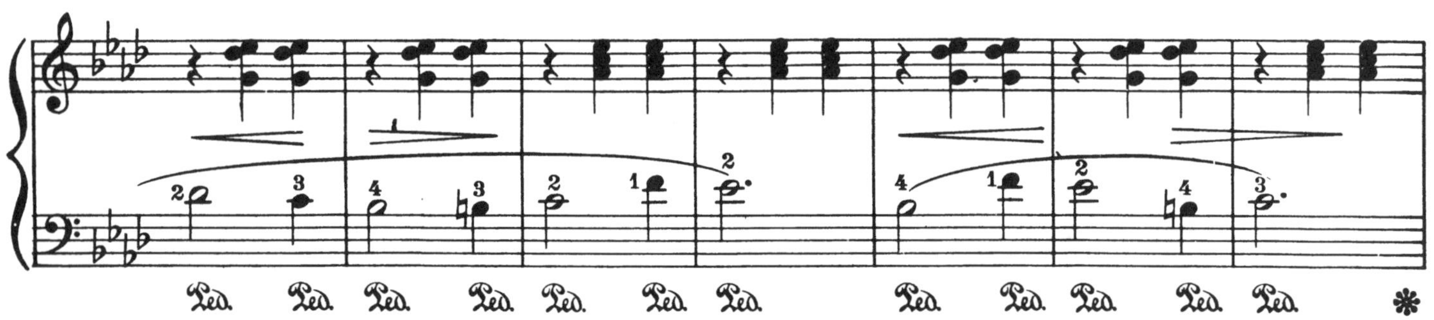

rit.
a tempo
cresc.
dim.
p
cresc.
f
dim.
mp

Under the Rose - Arbor

Theodora Dutton

dim. e rit. - - -
a tempo
mf
f
mf
f dim. - - - - -
pp
mf

Blue Danube Waltz

Edited by Carl Deis

Johann Strauss
Arranged by L. Streabbog, Op. 86

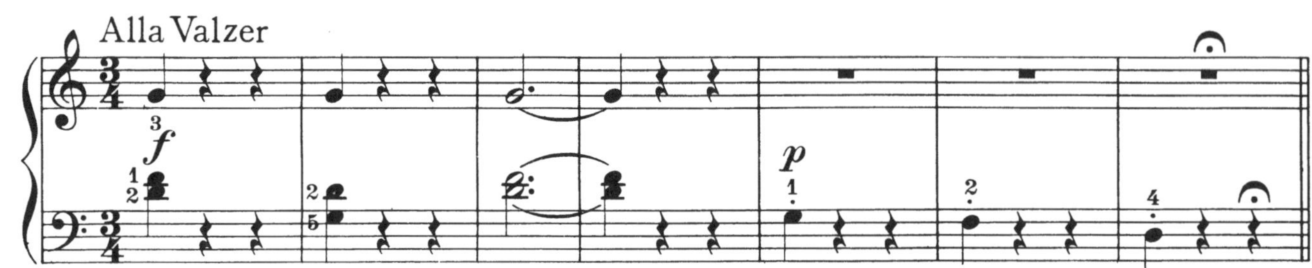

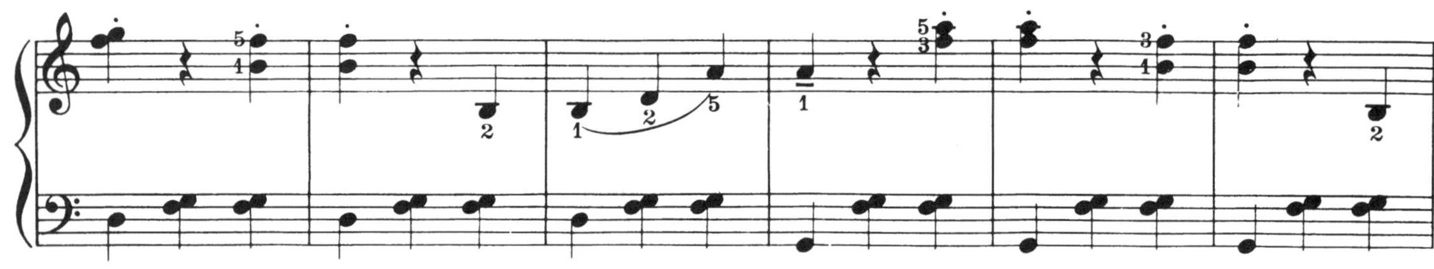

f
ff
p
f
p
f
fz

poco rit.
a tempo
p
a poco a poco cresc.
f
ff
p

cresc.
or easier:

mf
f
p
Coda
f
p
poco rit.

p
a tempo
a poco a poco cresc.
f
ff

Elfin Dance

EDVARD GRIEG. Op. 12.

Ped. come sopra

f pp

f pp

cresc.

f

pp

fz

fz pp

ppp

Minuetto giocoso

Edited and fingered by
Louis Oesterle

Joseph Haydn

cre -
ben marcato
- scen - do
delicato
Fine.
Trio.
I. volta mf
II. volta p
marcato
brillante
mf
*) or

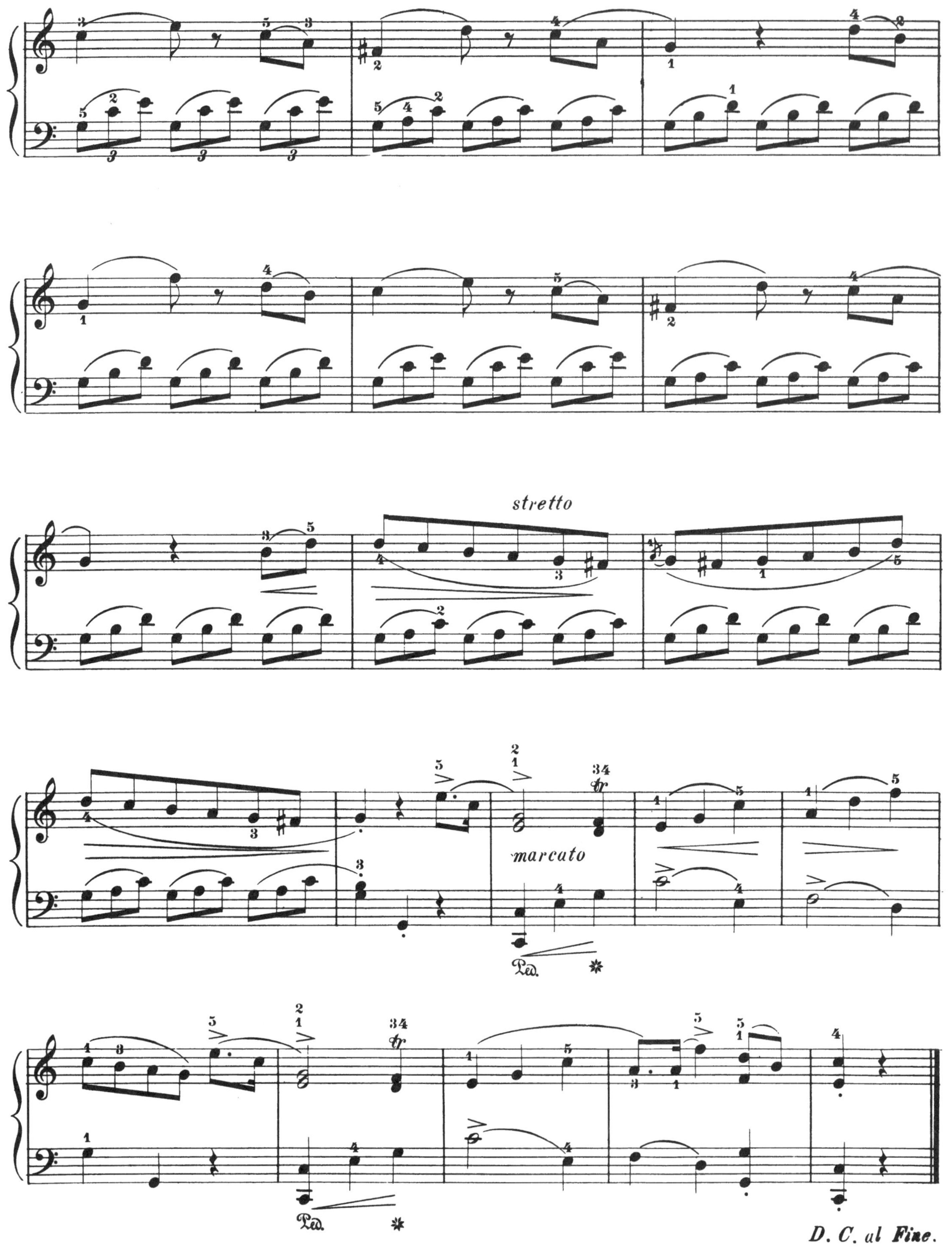
stretto
marcato
Ped.
Ped.

D. C. al **Fine**.

In the Gipsy Camp

Edited and fingered by
Louis Oesterle

Franz Behr, Op. 424, No. 3

p
Ped.
mf
f
marcato

a tempo
riten. un poco
pp
mf
f

p
grazioso
mf
p
f
un poco più lento
p
riten. un poco
a tempo
pp

mf
f
ff
ffz
ff
ffz

Pipes of Pan

Evalie M. Fisher

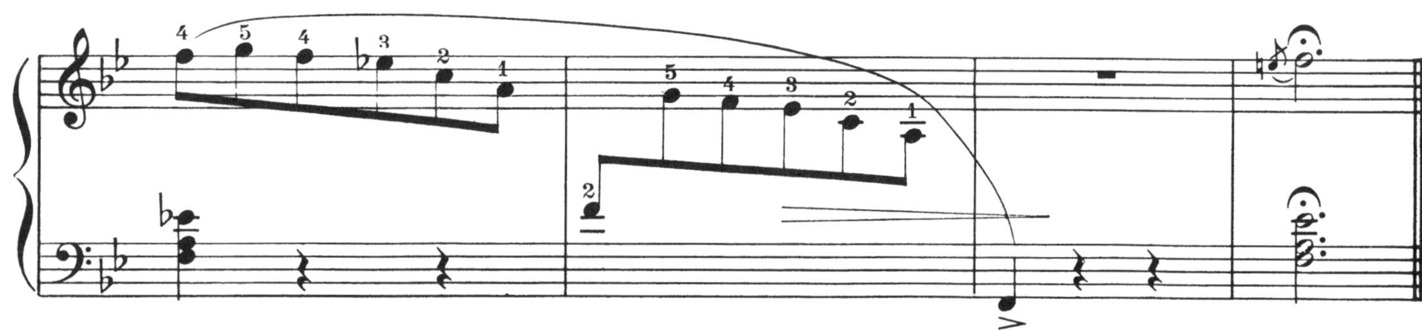

cresc.
mp
mp
rit.
p a tempo

f
rit.
a tempo
f

pp
mp
mp
p

mp
p
mp
cresc.
mp
p
mp

Toccata

Edited by
Edwin Hughes

Pietro Domenico Paradies
(1710-1792)

p
cresc.
f
fp
cresc.
f
p
cresc.
sf
p
f
molto stacc.

p subito
cresc.
f
fp
cresc.
1.
f
p
poco rit.
f
2.
f
mf cresc. molto
ff
rit. molto
sff
8

Albumblatt

"Für Elise"

Edited by Carl Deis

Ludwig van Beethoven

mf
dim.
a tempo
dim. e rit.
pp
dolce
cresc.
dim.
p
p

a tempo
dim. e poco rit.
pp
mf
dim.
p
dim. e rit.
a tempo
pp
p
cresc.
f
dim.
p
cresc.
f

dim.
p
pp
cresc.
dim.
a tempo
pp rall.
mf
dim.
p
dim.
pp
morendo

Serenade
Ständchen

Revised and fingered by
Wm Scharfenberg

Franz Schubert
Transcribed by
Stephen Heller

p
p
f
mf
pp
cantando

pp
p
pp
mf
p
p
f
Ped.

cresc.
fp
p dolce
f
f
decresc.
perdendosi
pp
dim.

Rustic Dance

Edited and fingered by
Louis Oesterle

C. R. HOWELL

sf
rit.
f a tempo
p

f
Ped.
p
Ped.
f

Ped.
ff accel.

From a Birch Canoe

Richard Bender

rit.
a tempo
poco cresc.
rit.
pp

Tarantella

Edited and fingered by
Albert von Doenhoff

Paul Beaumont

p leggiero
p

f
m.d.
m.s.
Prestissimo
ff sempre
fz

To Sally Jane Harris

Two Butterflies

Myra Adler

l.h.
Chasing one another
r.h.
pp
f
8va
Ped.
p
cresc.
accel.
a tempo

Lose Blätter.

Flying Leaves.

Edited and fingered by
Louis Oesterle.

Carl Kölling. Op. 147, Nº 3.

fz
fz
fz
fz
f

ff
Ped.
Ped.
Ped.
Ped.
Ped.
Ped.
Ped.

p
f
dimin.
p
cresc.

ff
Ped.
Ped.
Ped.
Ped.
Ped.
Ped.
Ped.
f
8

Prelude

Edited and fingered by
Rafael Joseffy

F. Chopin, Op. 28, No. 6

sostenuto
pp
ppp
Prelude
Edited and fingered by
Rafael Joseffy
F. Chopin, Op. 28, No. 7
Andantino
p dolce
Klindworth

Venetian Boat-Song No. 2

Felix Mendelssohn, Op. 30, No. 6

f
ff
sf
dimin.
pp
sf
dimin.
p
p
cresc.
al
f
dim.
p
cresc.
al
f
sf
dim.
sf
p
dim.
pp

None but the lonely heart

Nur, wer die Sehnsucht kennt

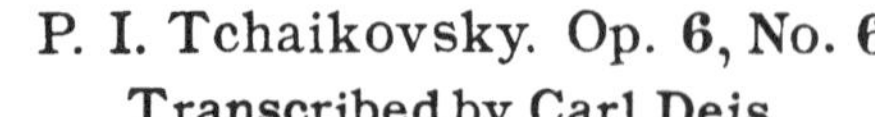
P. I. Tchaikovsky. Op. 6, No. 6
Transcribed by Carl Deis

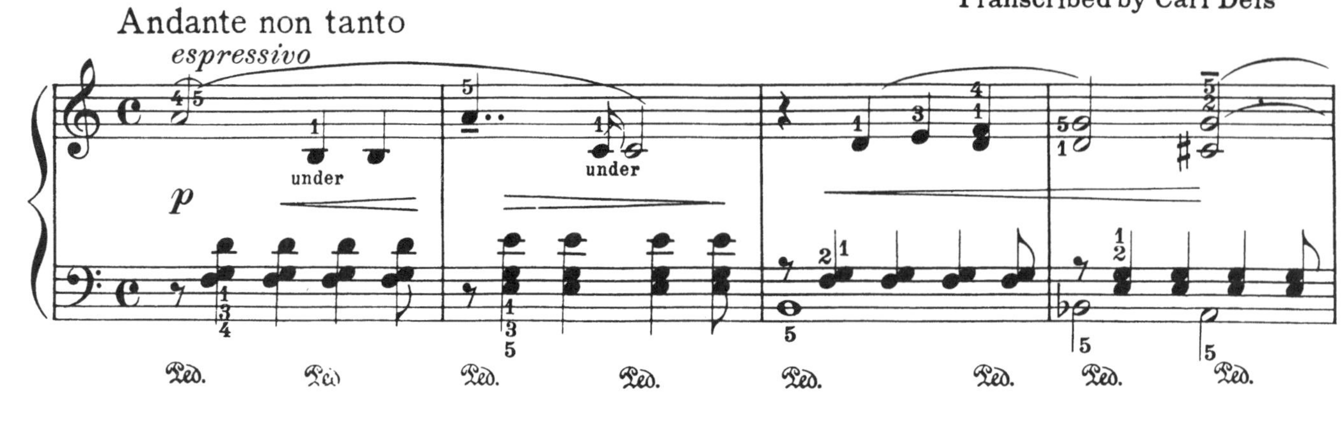

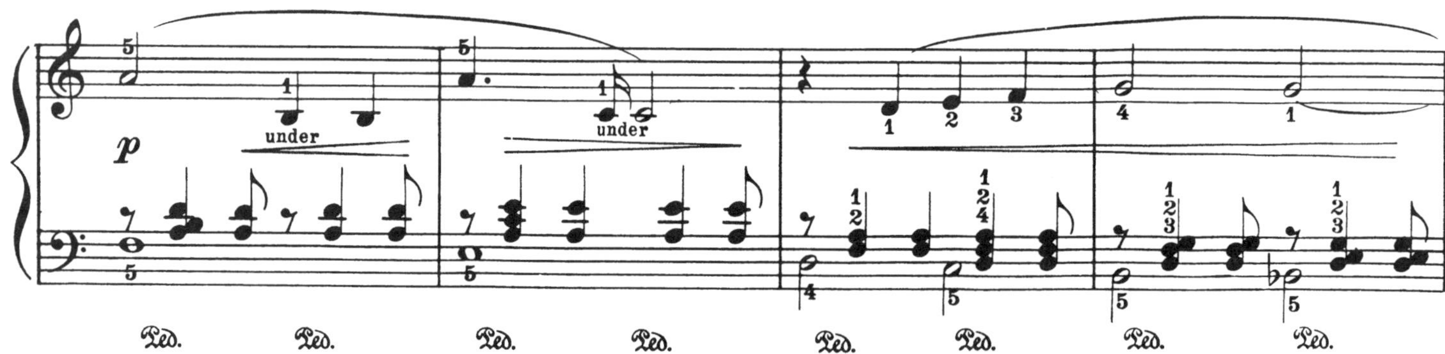

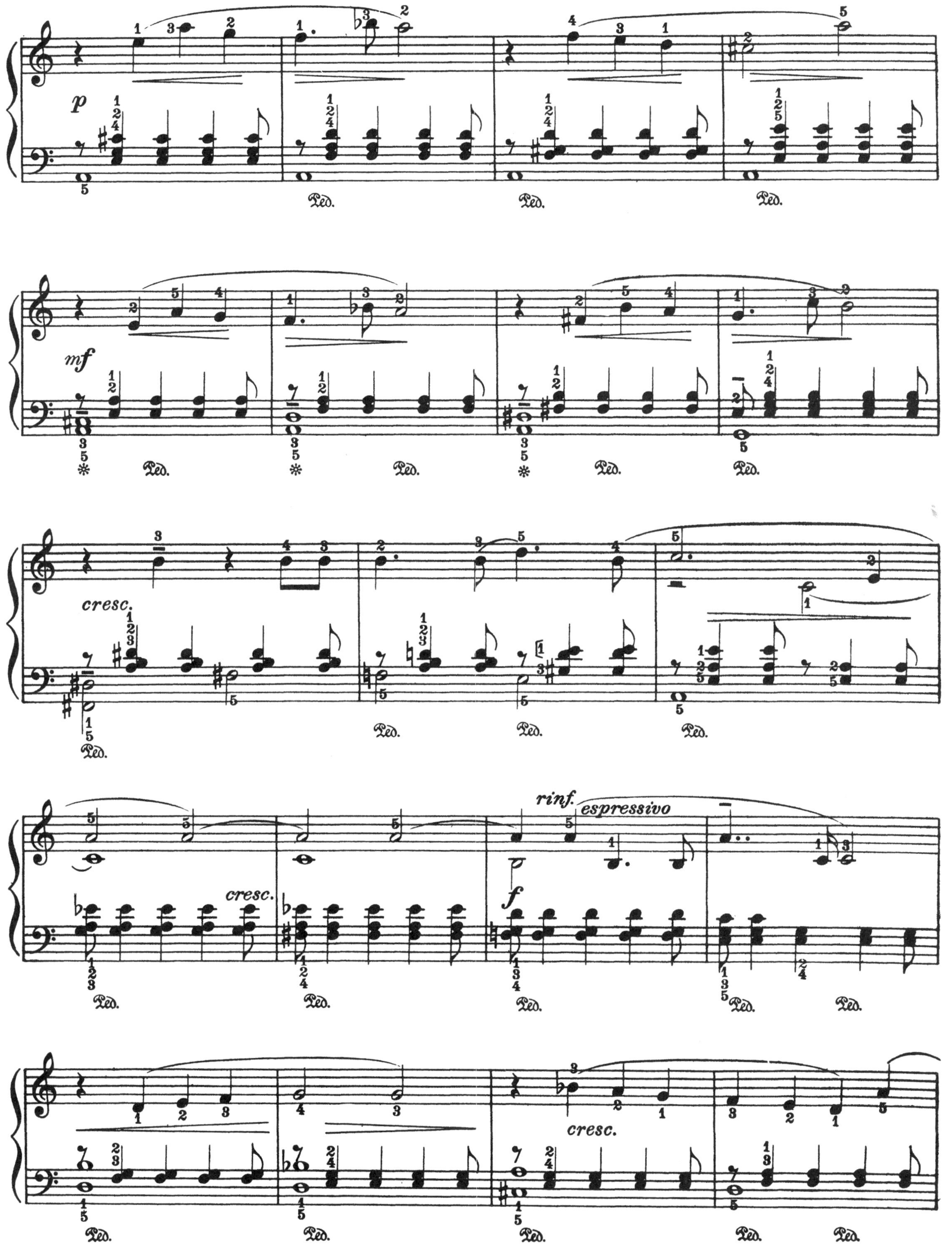
p
mf
cresc.
cresc.
rinf.
espressivo
f
cresc.

f
cresc. e
poco stretto
sfz
ff
p
riten. molto
a tempo
mf
f
meno f
dim.
pp

Christmas
December

Edited and fingered by
Louis Oesterle

Peter I. Tchaikovsky
Op. 37a, No. 12

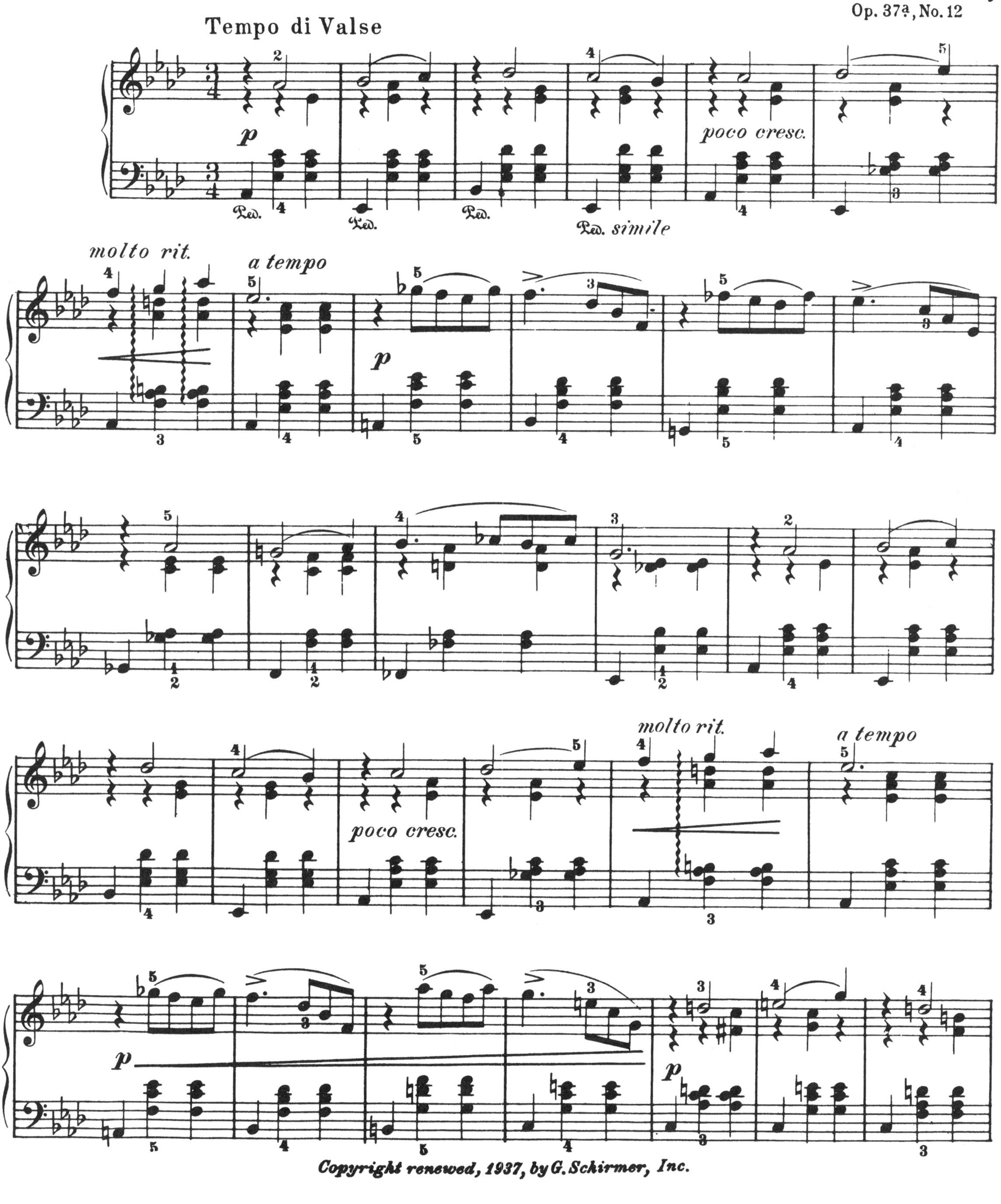

Tempo di Valse

p

poco cresc.

Ped. simile

molto rit. *a tempo*

p

poco cresc.

molto rit. *a tempo*

p

p
Ped.
mf
dim.
poco cresc.
Ped. simile
molto rit.
a tempo

molto rit.
a tempo
cresc.
mf
p
f
Ped.

p
poco cresc.
mf
p
poco cresc.
simile

molto rit.
a tempo
p
molto rit.
a tempo
poco cresc.
p
p
p

p
mf
Ped.
p
mf
dim.
p
molto rit.
a tempo
poco cresc.
Ped. simile
p
molto rit.

a tempo
p
cresc.
mf
p
poco a poco cresc.
f
mf

Le Tambourin

Edited and fingered by
Max Vogrich

JEAN-PHILIPPE RAMEAU
(1683-1764)

p
pp
pp
tranquillo
ppp sempre
poco rit.

As played by Fräulein Aus der Ohe

Berceuse
Lullaby

Revised and fingered Edition

A. Iljinsky, Op. 13

poco rall.
dim.
a tempo.
p
Ped.
una corda.
Ped.
dim. e rit.
pp

For M. B. H. R.

Cradle-Song

Wiegenlied

Johannes Brahms, Op. 49, No. 4
Arranged by Carl Deis

Dolce, con moto
Zart bewegt

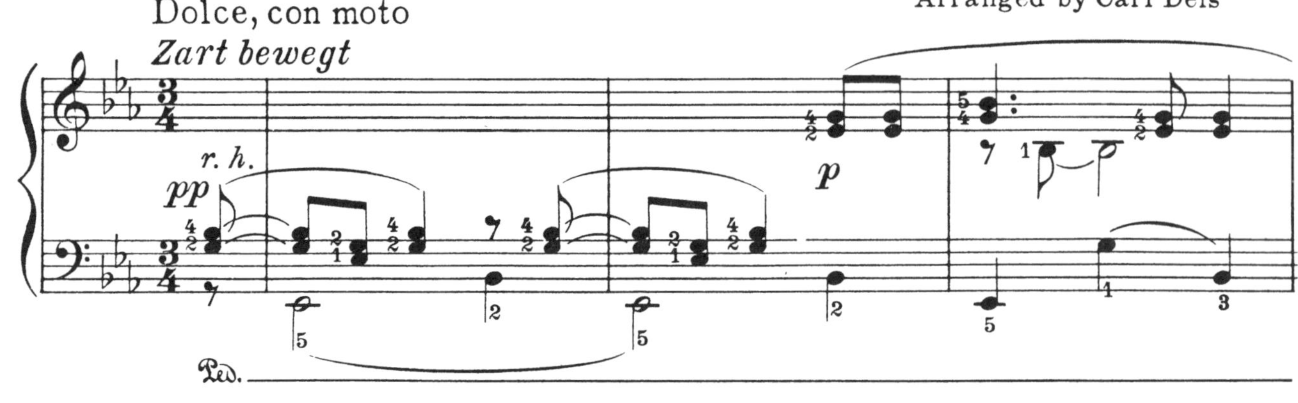

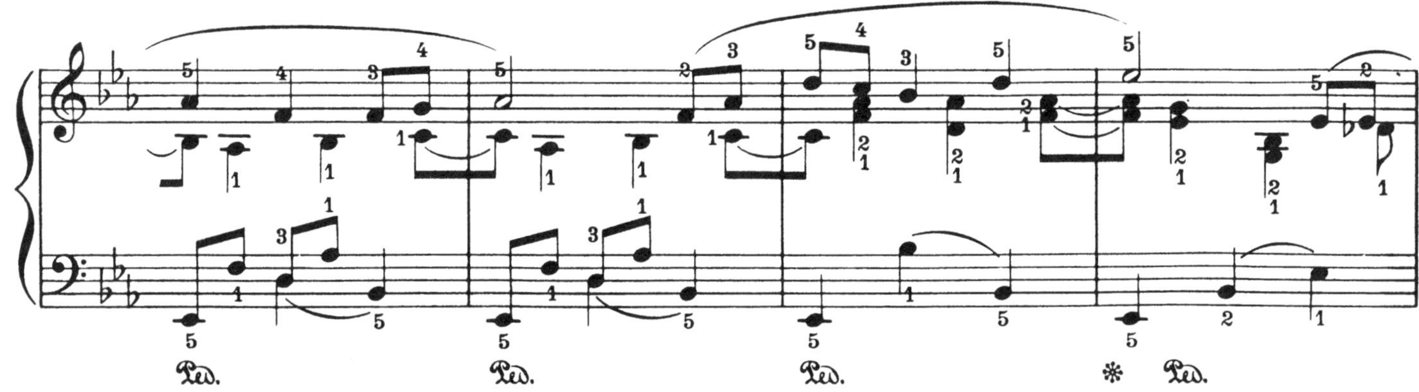

pp
r. h.
mf dolce
mp
pp
ppp
Ped.

Waltz

Edited by Carl Deis

Johannes Brahms, Op. 39, No. 15

dim.
(poco ritenuto - - - - - - -)
poco cresc.
(poco largamente - - - - - - -)
dim.
p dolce
(poco ritenuto - - - - -)

Simple Aveu
Simple Confession
ROMANCE SANS PAROLES

Revised and fingered by
Wm. Scharfenberg

FRANCIS THOMÉ

con anima
Animato un poco.
sempre marcato
calmato
poco rall.
Tempo I.
dolce

Animato con calore.
cre - - - scen - - do - poco - - a -
animato sempre
Tempo I.
- poco
f
con anima e marcatissimo il canto
Animato un poco.
mf e sempre marcato

calmato
diminuendo
poco rall.
Tempo I.
pp una corda
poco rall
pp a tempo
marcato il basso
ppp

Gipsy Rondo

(Hungarian Rondo)

by

Josef Haydn

Revised and fingered by
Wm. Scharfenberg

Transcribed by L. Köhler

cresc.
f
fz
fz
fz
fz
p
ff
p
ff
p
ff
p
ff

Minore I

Maggiore

p *cresc.* *fz* *fz* *p*

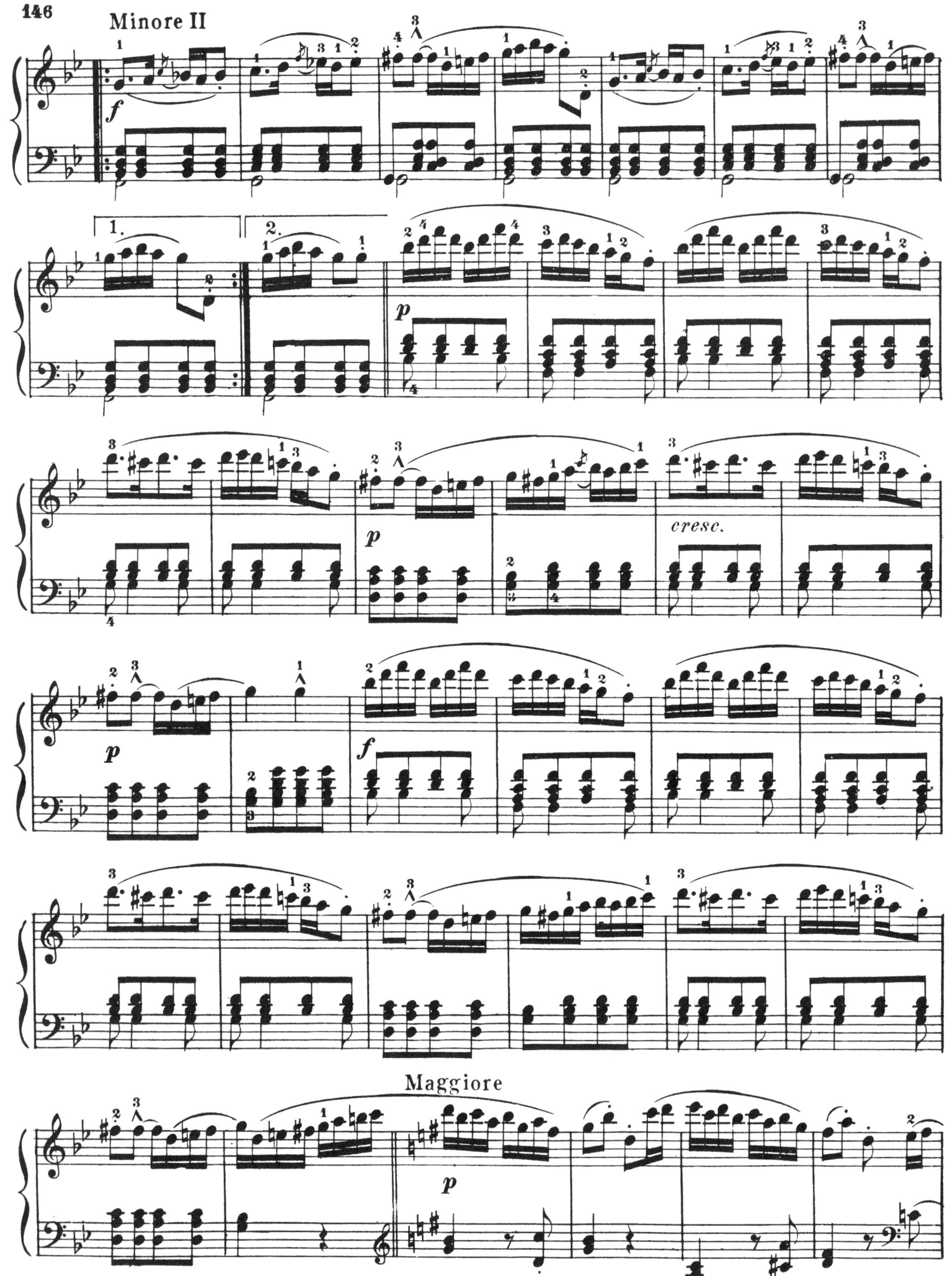
Minore II
f
1.
2.
p
p
cresc.
p
f
Maggiore
p

cresc.
fz
fz
f
dim.
p
f
fz
p
cresc.
f
ff

Pizzicati
Scherzettino

From the ballet "Sylvia"

Léo Delibes
Edited by Carl Deis

poco accel. e cresc.
a tempo
fz
fz
p
a tempo
poco rit.
p
p
poco accel. e cresc.
fz
fz

Tranquillo, l'istesso tempo
cantabile
p
p
mf

Come prima
p molto staccato
p
mf
a tempo
poco rit.
p
p
p
accel. e cresc. molto
ffz
ffz

Bridal Chorus

from the Opera

"LOHENGRIN"

Revised and fingered by
Wm Scharfenberg.

Richard Wagner
Arranged by Josef Löw

tranquillo.
p
Ped.
Ped.
Ped.
Ped.
Ped.
Ped.

p espressivo.
Ped.
cantando.
p
pp

pp
Ped.
p
dim.
mf
smorz.

Barcarolle

Intermezzo from the opera "Les Contes d'Hoffmann"

J. Offenbach

Ped.
dim.
rit.
2
2

Moderato
pp
molto cantabile

sempre più dolce
morendo
ppp

Au Matin

Revised and fingered by
Wm. Scharfenberg

Benjamin Godard

stringendo
rall.
cresc.
dim.
p
Ped.
a tempo
stringendo
rall.
m. g.
cresc.
dim.
p
Ped.
a tempo
un poco animando
cresc.
mf
Ped.
cresc.
rall.
a tempo
animando
f
p
cresc.
Ped.
rall. molto
mf
rall.
dim.
pp
Ped.

Tempo I.
cresc.
rall.
dim.
p
a tempo
cresc.
rall.
m. g.
dim.
p
a tempo
cantando
cresc.
rall.
ff
a tempo
dim.
con fantasia
p
rall.
pp

a tempo
Ped.
Ped.
Ped.
Ped.
Ped.
cresc.
Ped.
Ped.
Ped.
Ped.
rall.
a tempo
ff
dim.
Ped.
Ped.
Ped.
con fantasia
p
rall.
pp
Ped.
Ped.
Ped.
Ped.
a tempo
tranquillo
Ped.
Ped.
cresc.
Ped.
Ped.
dim.
Ped.
p
Ped.
Ped.

cresc.
rall.
a tempo
mf
dim.
pp
cresc.
dim.
tranquillo
p
pp
m. g.
cresc
dim.
pp

The Busy Saw-mill

For special study in interlocking of hands

Mathilde Bilbro

* Slide the fingers from the chord A sharp - D sharp to the Chord B-D natural. Notice measures 11 and 12.

(The busy mill sings a song)
mf
p
p
(Hurry up! there's work to do!)
f
p
f
p
legato
mf
pp

pp
pp
p
p
poco cresc.
p
p

Schmetterling.

Butterfly.

Edited and fingered by
Louis Oesterle.

Gustav Merkel. Op. 81, № 4.

sf
p
Ped.
cresc.
f
dimin.
p
cresc.
8
f
dimin.

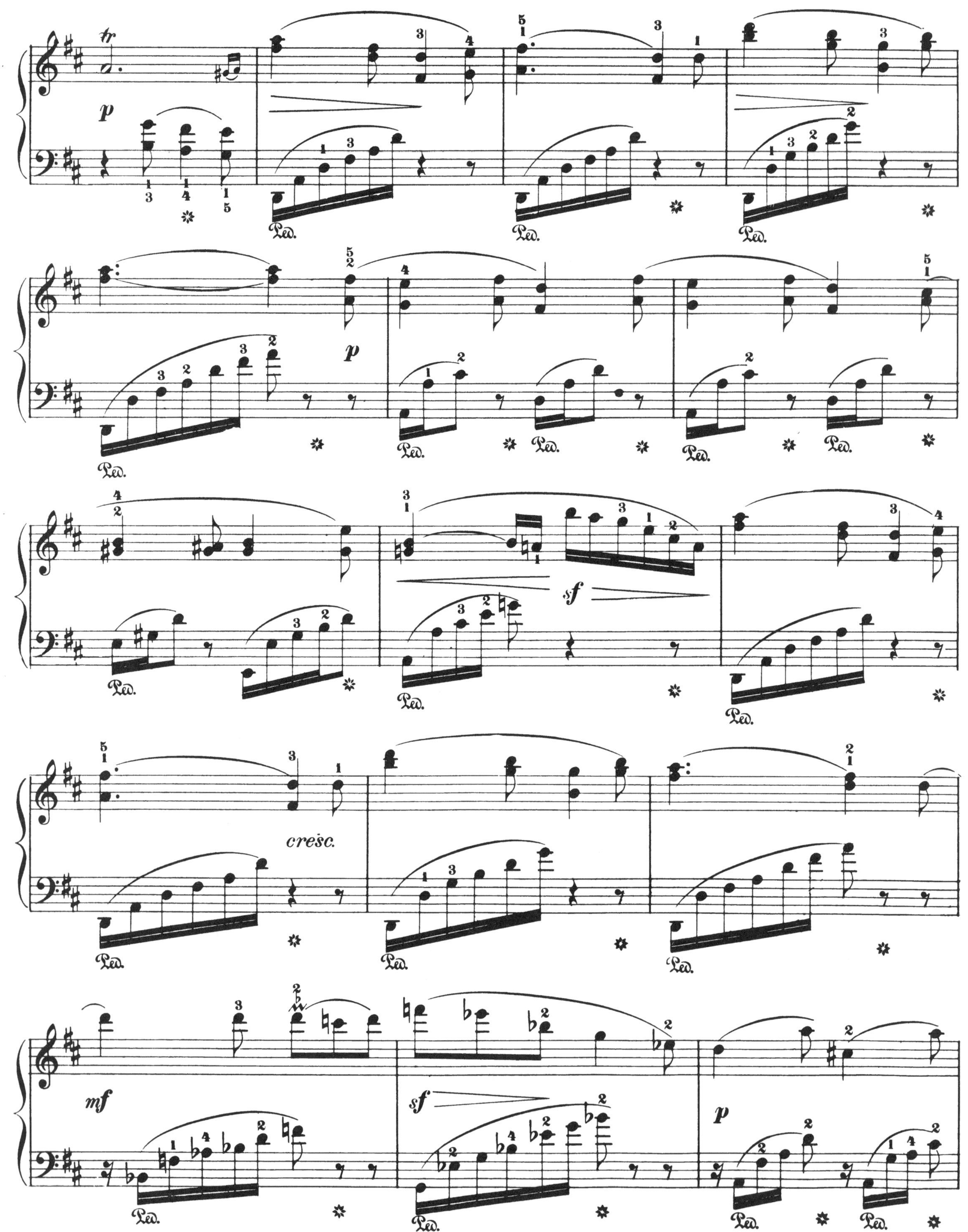

tr
p
Ped.
p
sf
cresc.
mf
sf
p

cresc.
mf
f
Ped.
sf
8
f.

2me MAZURK.

Revised and fingered by
Wm Scharfenberg.

BENJAMIN GODARD.

cresc.
mf
cresc.
ff
p
p
cresc.
animato.
rallentando molto.
ff
dim.
a tempo.
pp

cantando e legato.
cresc.
con fantasia.
dimin.
cresc.

con fantasia.
dimin.
pp
cresc.
dimin.
cresc.
dimin.
ff
ff

ff sempre.
p
p
f
p
sf
p
f

f
ff
ff sempre.
pp

cresc.
dimin.
pp
cresc.
mf
dimin.
pp
cresc.
f
dimin.

pp
p
p
f
p
f
f
p
pp
sf
animato.
fff
8

Dark Eyes

Russian Folk-Song

Transcribed by Richard Benda

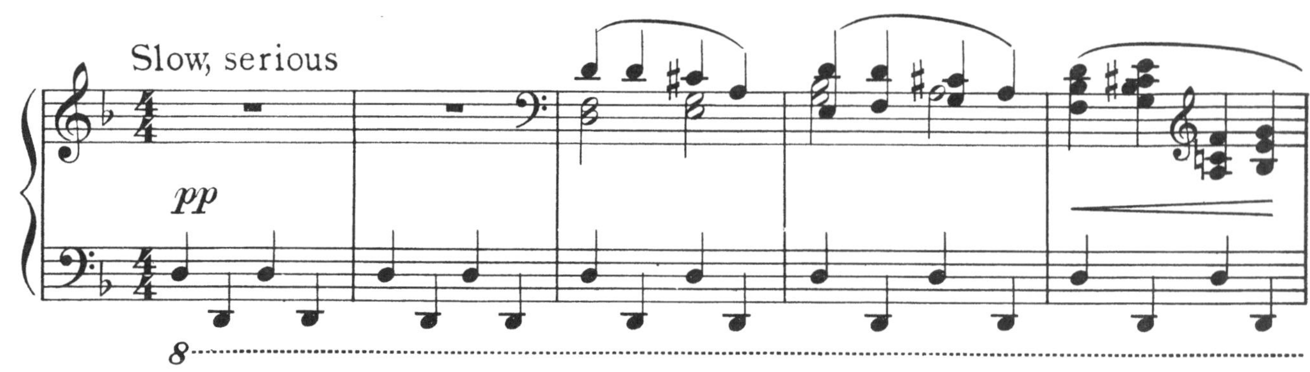

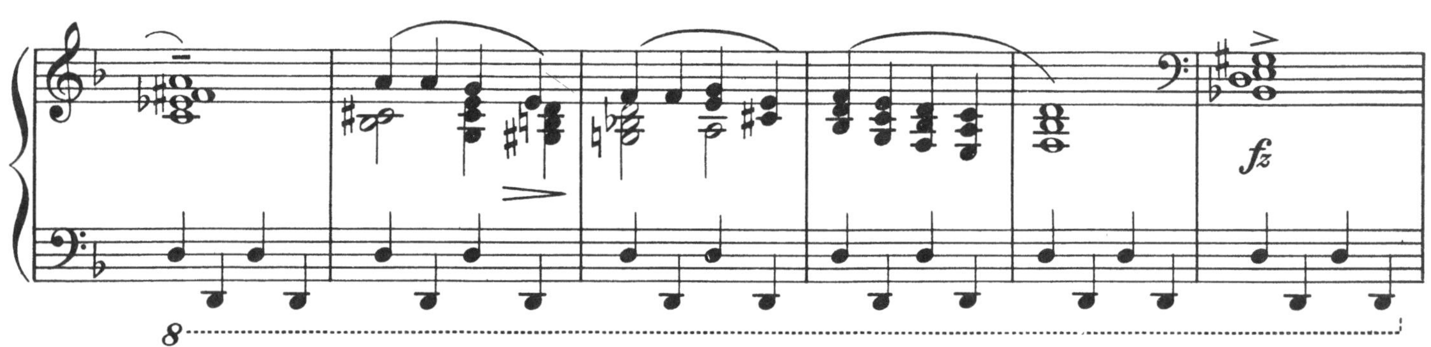

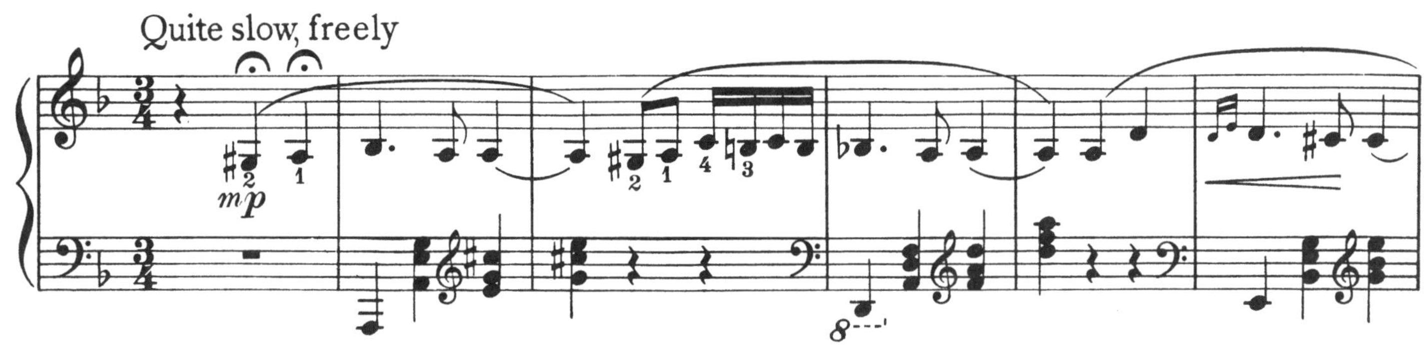

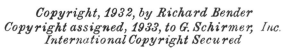

More movement
broad
Hold back
rit.

Spirited
f
Ped.
faster
p
7
solid
ff
l.h.
r.h.
broadly
freely

faster
cresc.
f
passionately
ff
mf
dim.
mp
dim.
p
As at first
pp
fz
pp